CW00519678

sea·change

sea·change

AN EPIC POEM

Jessica Streeting

propolis

First published in 2021
by Propolis Books

The Book Hive,
53 London Street,
Norwich, NR2 1HL

Jacket by Niki Medlik at **studio medlikova**

A CIP record for this book
is available from the British Library
ISBN 978 1 91690 511 5

Designed and typeset by benstudios.co.uk

Printed and bound by TJ Books Ltd,
Padstow, Cornwall

www.thebookhive.co.uk

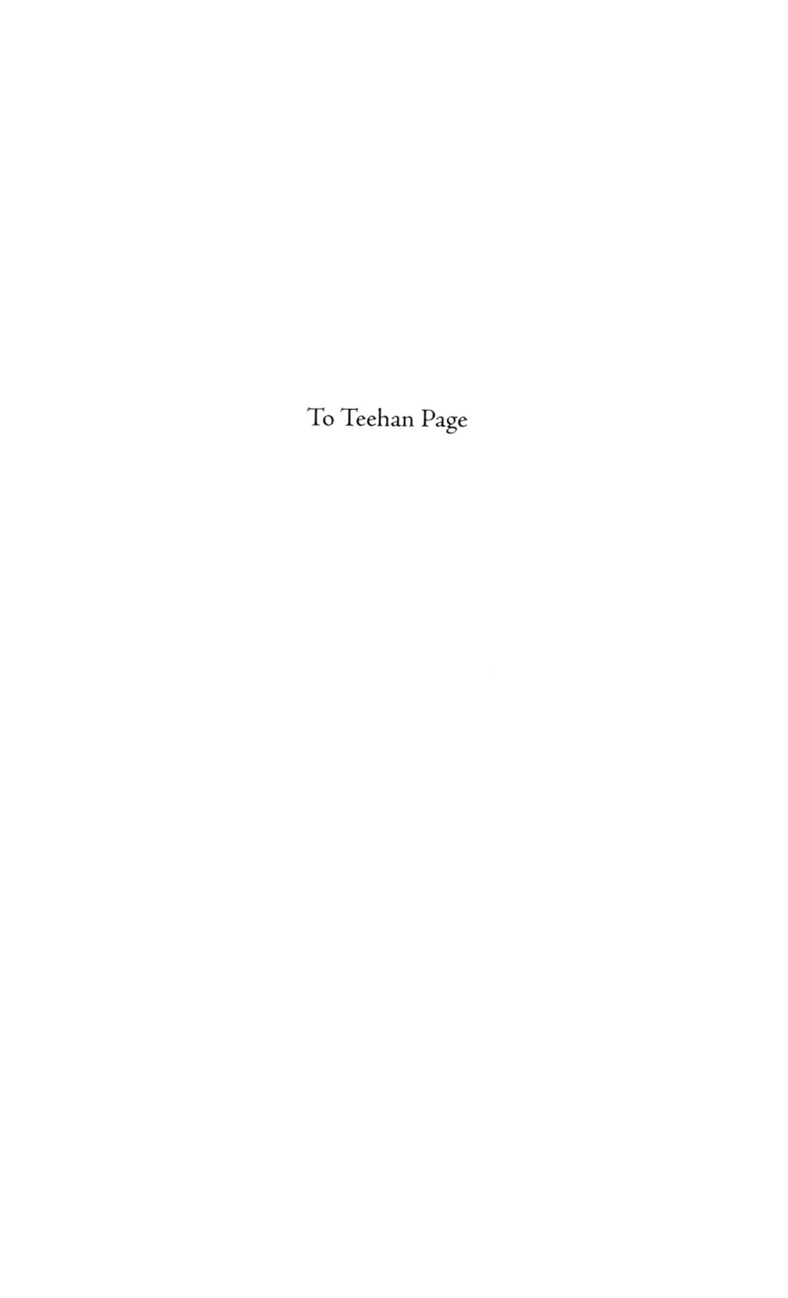

To Teehan Page

Foreword
by Stephen Fry

What a title!

It can sound facetious or trivial to compliment a writer or artist on their choice of name for a work. Yet the best titles – like a crown – can sanctify, seal and consummate. Could *The Wasteland* ever be what it is under another name?

I'll return to the perfection of the title in a moment. But first I have to warn you that I cannot encounter this remarkable poem as an innocent reader. I am *involved* here.

Jess Streeting's story begins with a dream: Dad (later identified as the Reverend Paul Farnham), responding to what appears to have been some kind of vision or calling, uproots his family (wife and two daughters, the elder of whom is our narrator poet) from a settled life in Oxfordshire, installing them in a vast and ageing Jane Austen Georgian parsonage in the village of Cawston in Norfolk. A far-flung spot, as remote as the living to which the 19th century divine Sydney Smith was sent, and which he famously characterised as being "...so far out of the way that it was actually twelve miles from a lemon."

We are in the 1970s, but the unbroken continuity of incumbents to the early medieval church, the isolation of rural Norfolk – farther by far from the madding crowd than

Thomas Gray's Stoke Poges country churchyard ever was – all combine to give the poet and us the impression that we are closer to the nineteenth than to the twentieth century.

I can vouch for the accuracy of this. I know. For as it happens, Paul Farnham and family, in landing in Cawston, landed just one mile down the lane from the house in which I grew up in the neighbouring, and even smaller, village of Booton.

The arrival of Paul Farnham was the realisation of a dream for me. I finally had a companion with whom I could talk books, ideas, music, logic and religion, an intellectual and spiritual mentor or – in the words of Alexander Pope – a "guide, philosopher and friend". For a long period barely a day passed without me walking or cycling down to the Rectory (they soon moved out of the Jane Austen parsonage and into the new purpose built Rectory that Jessica so exquisitely evokes) to spend time with this fascinating, engaging, eccentric, brilliant, beguiling man. He put me in the church choir as a bass, quite overlooking the tuneless mess I made of every note. He cast me in a production that he mounted of the Charles Williams verse play *Thomas Cranmer of Canterbury*. He even appointed me maths tutor to his daughters Jess and Alice. It was typical of his cast of mind that he should reason that I – as one who had all his life hated maths, fought against maths, resented maths, claimed an immutable maths "block" – would make a much better and more understanding teacher than someone for whom maths had always come easily.

Indeed Paul did zip around the green lanes of Norfolk on a whining scooter, or in a decommissioned London taxicab, just as Jessica describes, black gown and black hair flowing behind him. He looked strikingly like Jason Miller, the actor who played Father Karras in the film of *The Exorcist*, which was being banned from cinemas all round Norfolk at exactly this time.

This foreword isn't supposed to be about me, but I cannot help jumping up and down to tell you how magnificently perfect is Jess's evocation of place and time here. The Greeks have the word *nostos* – to describe the hero's journey home. But *nostos* is always so much more a *time* than a place. The pain we feel for the loss of that home we once had is *nost-algia*, home-pain. The primal *nostos* poem is of course Homer's Odyssey, a dangerous sea voyage from Troy to Ithaca. *Sea-Change* is a *nostos* poem *par excellence*. Which returns us to the title. Ariel sings this in *The Tempest*:

> Full fathom five thy father lies,
> Of his bones are coral made:
> Those are pearls that were his eyes;
> Nothing of him that doth fade,
> But doth suffer a sea-change
> Into something rich and strange

Those last three lines are carved on the tomb of Percy Shelley, who drowned at a young age. I shan't spoil Jess's story – for this is a narrative poem and what happens is unfolded so superbly that it would be an insult to short-circuit the telling – but the sea encircles this poem just as it encircles much of Norfolk, and the title hangs above the story as doves hover

over the composition of renaissance religious paintings, and "lifelike" angels look down on the congregants in the nave of Cawston Church.

You don't need to have grown up under the shadow of Rydal Mount in the 1780s to know and understand the truth of Wordsworth's *The Prelude*, and you don't need to have grown up in 1970s Norfolk to know and understand the truth of Jessica Streeting's *Sea-Change*. The poem reads with novelistic, almost cinematic narrative drive and clarity. It is beautifully written, beautifully sad, beautifully rueful, beautifully insightful and beautifully strong. It sings of bewilderment, love and loss. Poetic memory can raise the dead past, transforming it into something rich and strange indeed.

Stephen Fry 2021

Sea-Change

This Gate

Our world began with Dad's dream.
Life woke us up through a dream and our childhood became
Garden, fields, space
And more garden
And sea.
Music and play and more fields and more music
And sea
And sky.

Because people who write about Norfolk will always say sky.
"There always is sky," said my sister.
"Why mention sky?"
Then we moved and saw that
Sky takes up more space in Norfolk.
Important, the sky.

The dream was a portent of what was to come
And to bring us around
To the here and the now and the always.

In after witness
I need to think deep like the sea
Or a solo viola.
But my thoughts become strewn and then tumbled,

Capsized and cold.
And one April day,
Both an end and beginning,
We walked up the shore like ghosts,
Having left half our souls in the water.

We are not ghosts.
Both our parents have died now
And on they have gone.
"Well, most people have you know"
Dad would say, laughing.
To a shore that is other, a life that is greater,
So they are not ghosts.
In the rustling of leaves and the wondering here by the gate,
I might hope to see ghosts.

Children play in the gardens
Here, next to the church.
More homes have been built,
Which makes sense.

We were one stray,
Set-apart family
In acres of garden,
Our echoing Rectory
And one clergy stipend.

Midwinter

Just days since mum died.
I had gone to put flowers on dad's grave
In the cemetery.
Up by the bowling green.

I never stay long.
An awkward 'Hi Dad'
As gauche as that person of thirteen who saw him last.
He was all about afterlife
Rather than human remains.

So I wonder why I have come
And I scurry off
Sharpish.
He is not there and he is
As is everyone's graveside experience.
His body was there.
He is not and he is.

Lying safe in the cemetery,
Peaceful between
School and church,
Surrounded by village.

Then I walked down to this churchyard
Where no one got buried for centuries.
Time passes

Here by the tower of the
Gentle great church of
Saint Agnes.

This place is called
Cawston.
In a county of churches,
Fine, rich and faded
Just one looks like this.
Less graceful than Salle rising over the fields.
Precipitous, turret-free roof;
"They forgot the top, Dad."
"Well, maybe they did.
That's a thought."

Mr Kett our headmaster said the turrets for Cawston
Were smuggled to Salle
Through an underground passage.
He was careful to stress this was rumour.
Rumour be gone, we were off
Searching tunnel trails,
Crop patterns,
Trapdoors to underworlds.

"You must bear in mind that a tunnel was wildly expensive to
dig.
It is most unlikely…"
Mr Kett said, with a twinkle.

So why did our church though so tall
Have this unfinished look?
No spires.
We were dreamy,
With boundless imagining
Mr Kett knew.
He suggested and we were suggestable.

This place called Cawston.
We lived, we belonged for a brief time,
For a tiny beat of a wing.

The birds are so
Noisy and nosy.
I stare at the gate in the wall,
Our go-between.
Church through to Rectory,
Rectory to church
Gate always open.

A robin arrives on a plaque by a tree.
Always a robin.
'In memory of church warden Arthur,
Beloved wife Nellie.'

The robin cocks his head.

Remember the Brambles, Arthur and Nellie?

"Of course," I reply. "They were integral".

"Why are you here, stranger lady?"

Out loud to the clever, inquisitive robin I reply:

"I belong here like you do. I am no stranger to Cawston."

I talk to birds.
Grief has deranged me.
I stand by the gate to our garden.
A home, an eternal place, our
Little Gidding.

I stare, stupid, stupefied.
Everything still now
Where we were so busy.
The robin flits off.

We learnt poetry with
Mr Jack Kett.
Poetry, folklore and folk songs
And history, naturally.
Natural history.
How the now of our seventies Norfolk
Might fit to the past.
With Cawston the centre,
Cawston the heart of our world.

The village was central
And we took for granted that
Here was a learned and interesting man,

To nurture us all,
Like the rare fairy foxgloves
He showed us one warm afternoon.

We were a ramshackle bunch.
Our flat deadpan faces recited as
One Norfolk schoolchild

"Oot a be in Englund
Now that Aprul's hare"

In June.

But Mr Kett had hope in us,
Taught us to listen and look,
So that later we might absorb words and the music of words.
So we might return later
With poems in our heads
And the habit of happiness.

Smugglers holes
Duel stones,
Underground passages,
Spires that got smuggled by night.
And the highwaymen riding,
All sent us flying into fields
On our Saturdays,
Wild to discover the next brooch or
Axe head,

Up to the old inn door.
The Rat Catchers Inn.
"Brilliant name for a pub"
Said Dad.

"The tunnel would start at The Rat Catchers,
Wouldn't you think, Mr Kett?"
"You must keep in mind, children,
Tunnels were pricey to build..."

Our correct Mr Kett linked us to yesterday,
Helped us to know we had place,
No more but no less than each other.
Those of us born in the village
And those who, by happiest accident
Had just arrived,

"Fairy foxgloves
Not native, but naturalised;
First brought to Cawston by pastor and naturalist
Reverend Theodore Marsh.
The legendary Reverend
Theodore Marsh,
Our own eminent Victorian."
Said Mr Kett.

Our class trooped down from school as part of a nature walk,
Rose pink star flowers,
Tucked up by the wall,

Just through this gate,
By the beech tree.

I felt proud because this was our garden
And shy at what others might think.
Rectory families know homes are just lent
For a season,
Not owned.
Not native, but naturalised.

We were astonished to have found ourselves here
After Dad's dream,
Such a turn in our luck to be here
In the summer of seventy-five,
Sun warming the walled Rectory garden,
Even dark corners,
Where toads lurked and small flowers flourished.

Reverend Marsh was the rector
For fifty Victorian years,
His nephew succeeded him,
As was often the way.
Fifty years, five years, five hundred.
Time stretches were meaningless
Only the seasons made sense
And we were in summer,
High summer.

"What's a rector?"
Asked someone.
Clustered around,
Underwhelmed by the dusty old plants,
Rectors were not normal people
But were other.

A Rector was travelled and learned
And odd.
Pursued unusual interests for
Love of God.
Henry Marsh had brought foxgloves
One hundred years past.
What might this Rector bring?
Reverend Paul Farnham.
This one they might glimpse as he
Buzzed along between churches
On his bright red Vespa,
Black clergy cloak billowing.

This new one who brought to assembly
Strange musical instruments,
Elaborate metaphors;
"God's love might be seen in this way,
Do you see?"
This one
Who was also the Dad of these
Funny new kids.

In this way Mr Kett encouraged acceptance
Of my sister and me.
The new Rector's children,
With different clothes and un-Norfolk accents;

"Are you Scottush?"
"No, we're from Oxford"
"From Oxford!"
"They're Scottush.
Ordyordyordy!"
They had circled us in the school field,
Chanting their mystifying;
'Ordyordyordy',
With the notion that we were from Scotland.
"We're not!
We are not, are we Jess?"
"No, we're not, Alice! Of course not."

They were curious, not mean.
But soon they were not even curious.

We slotted in,
Made our new ways of talking,
As new children have always done.
'Norfolk' for playground,
What they called 'posh' for at home,
In-between way
For Mr Kett,
Who was not to be fooled.
And whose wife was from Scotland.

Mr Kett wrote a book he called
Yesterday's Children;
Imaginary stories from far back in time,
Around real events.
He connected the children of yesterday
To ourselves.
Back then we were only so interested
In a book.
These stories he wove
Into the fabric of our everyday.
Wool trade and weaving and
Plough boys and duelling.

Mr Kett was an oral historian,
Stories spun into maths,
Comprehension
Singing Together.
He spoke poetry in Norfolk, wrote books of nature,
Made everything rhyme in his poems,
Illustrated his neat, careful stories,
Even compiled our own efforts,
Typed out on sugar paper, stiffly titled;
'Our School Life.
'Cawston Celebrates
The Silver Jubilee'.

So we learned that
While living and playing in a village,
You could write.

You could chronicle life.
Mr Kett sowed these seeds.

The robin flits back
"All that was in summer"
He sings.

"Yes, in summer."

"Locked in time" he adds.

"Yes, I know".

"No fairy foxgloves on this winter's day
And that gate is locked."

But gently I push at the soft green lichened door,
Stories still lie behind gates,
Time can shift,
All is not as it seems.

"We are not in a fairy tale
Or silly poem.
We are not in a dream".
Scoffs the robin, off again,
Uncaring in the way of a bird.

I hear beating wings as drifted snow,
Children's laughter.
You silly old,

Middle-aged
Orphan.

This door
Will not open miraculously,
Or with a gentle push.
Then why is my hand on the latch?

The Ketts and the Brambles have died.

"Of course they have died,
They would be ancient by now
You can't live forever!" says the bird.

Dad died ages ago,
Now Mum.
And today I'm in liminal space

On the edge of the sea and the shore.

Both parents in mind
And those others who died,

All so near.
Speaking the language of heaven
The language of madness
The madness of
Hoping for heaven
From cold
Earth.

This is the gate to the world that
Dad dreamed
Then made our reality.
In sublime moments
Wires, golden wires run between us
And their immortal hearts.
Stretching up
Reaching down
Those golden wires
A dream vision.
Not today.

"Well tell us your tale if you must"
Says the robin,
Back on his branch.

"Do I have a tale to tell?"

"Don't we all?
Start here.
All good stories begin with a gateway.
And with an important robin,"
He adds,
Puffing his chest.

"A story to add to the tales of
Yesterday's children.
Tell the story
And start with the dream".

Another place

Dad dreamt that he sailed to an island,
Somewhere easterly,
Somewhere watery.
An angel-like figure had pulled his boat in
And led him up the beach.
A gate led from a vast church Dad did not know,
To a beautiful old house
And wild garden.
"You will bring your family here"
Someone had said,
Possibly God.

And then Dad had woken,
A warmth and a promise staying with him all day,
"As the best dreams make you feel, you know, children?"
"Yes, Dad."

"And the strangest thing"
We sat round his strong handmade table,
As he cupped his big hands round his beer,
"The extraordinary thing,
When the Bishop was showing me,
When we walked down the path together,
Before we went into the church
And looked up at the angels
I saw porch to the right

And the gate to the left.
Norfolk Angels wear feathery breeches,
You know."
"Do they, Dad? Like the Wombles?"
"Not unlike."

But after that, Dad explained,
"We walked through a gate
Into a beautiful garden and the strangest thing was
It was *the* garden,
The gate,
The church of my dream,
Do you see?
It was not an island,
Sea did not lap at the shore,
But in all other ways it was just like my dream.
And Norfolk is rather cut off,
Not unlike an island."

He had tailed off at this,
With a swift glance at mum,
Who we knew felt cut off already.

How would Mum feel for this strange, watery island of
Norfolk?
But mum listened calmly,
With no annoyed blink.
Our hearts rose,
As they do

When your parents seem suddenly unencumbered.
Mum said

"Coming home, in a way.
Did you know that Gar's family all come from Norfolk?
A market town,
Swaffham.
For me, it would be like returning," she smiled.

Dad had nodded, encouraged.
"There are churches with hammer beam angels
All over the county.
Swaffham less striking than Cawston, perhaps.
Those angels!"

He reached for mum's hand and she took it.
"Fifteenth century,
Untouched
And quite life-like."
He laughed, his eyes happy.

"Were the angels the same as your dream?" asked my sister.
"The strange angel who brought you to shore?"

Our parents had smiled at that too
In that good way that happens
When both parents love something you've said.
"That's a thought," said Dad.
"Possibly,

I couldn't look closely
And hadn't much time.
They are so far up,
High in the roof of the church.
Such a building!" Dad beamed and threw out his hands wide:
A great Norfolk barn of a place,
Full of faded
Medieval
Glory."

I heard hammer beaming angels
Strike in my head.
Come to Cawston.

"Upkeep?"
Mum raised half an eyebrow.
"Harder than Hitchin."
Hitchin was another parish
They had been to consider.
They had returned saying
"Hitchin's well healed"
Whatever that meant,
And with none of the joy Dad was showing tonight.

"Upkeep, yes a challenge," said Dad.
"But the village of Cawston is thriving.
There's a lovely small school,
I met the headmaster, whose name
Most incredibly, is Kett."

"Why most incredibly, Dad?"
"Robert Kett led the Norfolk Rebellion".
"Oh."
"Those angels were carved even earlier."

So many revelations in one evening,
With our toast and marmite.

Allowed to stay up until Dad was home,
We had sensed much at stake.
"Will we move to Cawston now,
After your dream, Dad,
After the angels?" asked Alice.
"Well, yes, if the Bishop and Mummy agree,
Then we might."

"Hooray!"

My little sister and I caught the joy,
Danced off in our nighties, barefoot
Round the one straggly rosebush.

Disaffection

Before Norfolk
We lived in a grey house
On a dry street.
Grey cement thrown at the walls
In a style which Dad had called
Pebbledash.
We saw no pebbles,
Just concrete dashed
On concrete.
Despite all this concrete
The house felt unstable
Like cardboard.
And damp.
It might not stay up,
Might blow down in one puff
If the big bad wolf were to pass by.

Dad's job was
A Chaplain at
The mental Hospital.

"What's mental, Dad?"
"The balance of our minds, darlings.
Sometimes people struggle,
Become ill,
Lose their balance."

"Do they ever get better, Dad?"
"Some do."

And some stay for years
Wobbly
Unbalanced,
Unstable
Waiting to be well.
In our road.

Dad could slip into Oxford to hear the choirs sing
And to dream in the spires.
Once he took me.

"The finest sound
In England now.
An electric extraordinary choir.
Simon Preston is
Organist and Choirmaster here at
Christ Church.
He is a genius
You will see."

Palm Sunday
With music called
Plain song.
We sat on the end of a pew
In the dark
Sunday building.

No folded palm cross
But an actual palm
Cutting into my fidgeting fingers.
They sang nothing that I could join in with,
The plain song went over my head.

Dad told me that
Were I a seven-year-old boy
Not a girl,
I might have auditioned to be part of this choir.
"I can sing just as well as a boy."
I had boasted, indignant.
"Dad, I can!"
Stopping short of
"It's so unfair!",
Unsure I would want to spend time
In that gloomy place,
Singing such plain old song.

Dad bought an old punt in Oxford,
Which he painstakingly renovated,
Varnishing wood to a shine,
Pushed us peacefully downstream near Sandford
With a little picnic,
Puffed on his pipe.

"Not sailing, but better than nothing"
He said.
"What is sailing Dad?" asked my sister.

"Read Swallows and Amazons.
Or perhaps you're too young."
I was seven and not a great reader,
Alice was four and reading already.
Dad was vague about what was
Expected of children
And never talked down to us.

Swallows and Amazons came out as a film
In time for my birthday.

We borrowed Gar and Grandpapa's Dormobile to fit all our
friends in.
Drove into Oxford to see the film.

After that, I pretended to tack
An imaginary boat
Through the scrubland

Behind the grey houses,
Under the shadow of
Cowley chimneys
Like Roger from Swallows and Amazons

I hoped.
I was trying to impress Dad,
As he wouldn't notice my singing.

And we learned way back
When Dad was a boy,

He had learnt to sail in Norfolk.
Sailing,
His boyhood passion.

I still didn't understand
Swallows and Amazons.

Better drowned than duffers.
If not duffers, won't drown.

"What's a duffer, Dad?"
"An incompetent person." said Dad, adding;
"I never liked that bit.
Sailing is tricky, even for competent people."
I hadn't asked what incompetent
And competent meant.
Too many questions broke
The natural peace of the river.

Another clergyman called Lyle came to visit
And sat in our punt, singing;
My cup's full and runneth over
Charismatically, tunelessly,
Lifting his hands in Praise,
Almost toppling the boat.
Lyle shattered the peace of the river
But Dad didn't mind, grinning
As he pushed us along,

This was the way of life.
Clergy unusual and Godward,
Our father, musical,
Lyle, not.

Mums were not clergy
And didn't get the time to punt round the river
Or swan off to Evensong.
"Do we live in Oxford, Mum?"
"We live on the outskirts"
"What are outskirts?"
"The edge."

We live on the edge.

"Look, dreaming spires!"
Alice took mum's hand
Pointed out steel pylons
Stretching out from outskirts
And down through the
Middle of England

An old soldier in a grubby white tank top
Marched up and down,
All day and into the evenings,
Swinging his arms,
Sometimes shouting commands.

"There goes Snow White, Mummy"
Alice called from the window.

"Bill White, darling."
"Snow white hair."
Alice traced her small hands down the windowpane,
Waved at Bill White
Bill White waved back.
"Can I go out and play with Bill White, Mum?"
"No darling, he's not a child."
"But he sings in the street Mum and
Mummy?"
"Yes darling"

"What does mental mean?"

Next door lived some patients
Deemed healthy enough
To live out of the hospital.
We were told that our neighbours
Would like little jobs,
To help them feel less on the edge.
So mum asked one lady called Mossie
With candy floss hair
To clean our house for money.

On Mossie's first day
Mum was teaching and we were at school,
Mossie knocked all the ornaments
Flying off our mantelpiece
And took flight.

We found mum crying.
"A tile was loose,
I should have explained."
"What's Mogadon Mum?"
"What's an overdose, Mummy?"
"Mossie wasn't very well."
And then more to herself than to us.
"This will not do."

Mum's piano leant
Up by the mantelpiece.

"Play your favourites Mum
Play Harmonious Blacksmith"
Whatever that meant.
"Play Sheep May Safely Graze."

So mum played the music of simple perfection
Deft, understated,
Restored order as mum always did.
And tears rolled down her cheeks
And we danced half-heartedly
Up and down,
Hoping for change.

But now Dad had dreamt up a change,
Heralded by a hammer beam angel.
We were moving in June
On Dad's birthday.

Our punt went ahead,
Majestically solo.
A bright yellow van had turned up in our road
Jarrett's of Norwich Removals.
Some poor hapless family
Were moving from Norfolk to
Outskirts.

Dad made a deal with the men,
So they took our punt back
In their empty van,
With the promise of coming back for us all.

"Where will the punt go until we arrive, Dad?"
"Outbuildings next to the Rectory."
Outbuildings, outskirts,
New words each day
When you are
Five and eight.

We were leaving our family behind,
Our grandparents and cousins
Who all lived
In the nearby,
Worlds away,
Cotswolds.

But we left with their blessing.
Gar's eyes lucid blue in her soft cushion face,

Had grown misty.
"Norfolk is magical, tinkers.
You're so lucky to be moving back."

"How can we move back somewhere
We've never been?
Silly Gar!"
"Why's Norfolk magic, Gar?"

"Sky" said Gar firmly, kneading lardy pastry.

"Sky and sea.

Sea and sky".

"But sky's everywhere, Gar!"

Sky is everywhere.

"Will you visit us, Gar?
Norfolk's a long way".
"Never heard of the National Express, kiddoes?
Just try stop me,"
Said Gar.

This way

Our journey would take hours and hours,
A long way for our car,
A retired London taxi
Which broke down every time we went anywhere.
Bicester, Buckingham,
Bedford, Beyond.
We had sweets,
Orange squash
And we squashed in with cases
And down tipped the rain,
As we trundled along behind
Jarrett's of Norwich Removals,
Dad smoking,
Mum driving.

Years later the road opened out
And we saw there was sky.
Twisted trees
Like The Cat in The Hat
Bent away from the sky.
Sky through the smoky wet window,
No sea.
Gar had said sea.
"But look how these trees bend right in from the wind
That comes straight off the sea."
Dad told us, so proud to be showing us his Norfolk land.

Mum bumped our car up to a pub
And Dad turned his big body towards us.
Luckily he wasn't driving today.
Driving did not always stop him from turning to chat.

"We are stopping for lunch,
The Bull Inn
Barton Mills.
We used to stop here when I was a boy."

"Stopping for *lunch?*"
"Yes. This is where Norfolk begins,
It's an old coaching inn."
"For our lunch in a *pub*!"
"Well, a hotel, but they might let us eat
In the lobby."
Stiff maroon velvet-bound menus
As big as our heads.
Children's menus were not yet invented.
Little Chef was a little behind us
In coming to Norfolk.

"Have whatever you want,
Perhaps you'd like gammon."
"What's gammon Dad?"
"Fat bacon. It comes with a pineapple ring."
"Gammon please"
"And me," said Alice.

Salt fatty meat,
Sweet soft yellow ring
In the same warm miraculous mouthful
Then back to the car for what dad called
The last leg.
A long leg then,
Like Dad's legs.
We passed from one side to another,
Through a fairy tale forest
Through fire
In my mind.

"Look now, a tall tower
With a pineapple perched on the top."
After lunch, this made sense.
A sand-coloured column
Topped by
The Norfolk Pineapple,
Which actually is an urn.

"It's a war memorial" Dad said.
"But also a
Forest-fire
Look-out tower".
This tossed casually in.
"Fire?"

To be swept off by flames high as fir trees,
In a wind that blows straight from the sea.

Burnt to crisps in our car
Before Norfolk began.
"Mum, Dad said fire!
Dad said *fire!*"
"Jess, its fine.
There's no fire,
No danger."
Not fine.
There was danger.
Our lives are at risk.
Why have a look-out post for no reason?
"Help!"

They didn't look round or race faster
To outrun the fire.
So uncaring.
They both smiled,
Laughing gently at me
And Dad had his hand on mum's knee.
And Alice unbothered,
How stupid they were.
Alice looked through the window
Unaware of her fate,
"There's no fire, Jess, don't worry."
How could she possibly know
At her age?

The patients would
Often set fire to their beds,

On the edge.
What an odd thing to do
Accidentally
Or for a purpose.
But it went with
Being mental.
Most days an alarm rang out,
Shrieked down our street.
Night-time sirens
Which terrified me
Out of my night mind.

I knew the fires would spread
Down our road
Right up to our pebble-dash walls.
So was often engulfed by my fear of the flames.

"Why darling?
Why are you frightened?
You don't need to worry" both parents would say.
"When we were young
In the War
Sirens meant bombs."

"And your house might burn down?"

"Well, yes
But ours didn't
And now there's no war and

No danger.
You don't need to worry."

Well I knew for certain
We were not safe,
But right on the edge of great danger.
I leaned through the gap in their seats
To get their attention,
To spell out what they were too stupid to see.
"But these trees are *wood,* Dad,
The fire could *spread*..."
"Jess, sit back now.
It really is fine.
And its pouring with rain."
Flames could chase,
Fire consume us.
I felt sick.
Gammon and pineapple churned
And the world all but ended.

Then I must have dropped off
And we drew up outside
The Bramble's bungalow.

Mr Bramble came out in his shirtsleeves,
His trousers high over his middle,
Braces tight over his tum.
Holding an umbrella at the window,
He leaned in

A chubby Mr Tumnus
Shaking raindrops off a
Whiskery face.

"Rector, Sir, Bor,
Mrs Farnham
Little 'uns."
He nodded to each of us,
Wide-awake now,
Transfixed by this story book man
With his soft Norfolk voice.
He said solemnly;
"Welcome to Cawston."
And handed Dad keys.

Dad thanked him,
Shook his hand through the window.
Mum laughed
And we loved that she laughed
And they both seemed so happy.
Delighted,
We bounced on our seats,
For the first glimpse of Cawston.

Down Back Lane, left into
New Street,
Sturdy square bungalows,
Might one be ours?
They looked solid

And warm
And would not blow down
Or burn.

And the rain stopped
And sunlight hit New Street.
They wound down their windows
And bumped up a drive,
Tipped us out of our car.

"Here we are.
Here's our church
And our Rectory
And the gate,
Like my dream, do you see?" Dad beamed.
"Its all our dream now, Dad."

Said Alice.

Rhapsody

Sun shone for the rest of the summer.
People talk of
Seventy-six,
For us it was seventy-five,
One light filled day
And quiet warm night.

An old empty house we could not hope to fill
With our furniture,
So never mind that.
Lots of room for our piano
Long echoing hall
And a landing so wide we could roller-skate
Up and down.
Cool, chalky cellar,
Long empty of wine,
Cobwebs running the length of the house,
Small, boarded attic rooms
For long gone servants,
Old school room,
Walls hung with chalk boards,
An airing cupboard large as a railway carriage,
A bathroom with two baths.
"How unusual," said Mum
Hugging Dad.

And two staircases,
One at each end.
A stone-flagged kitchen,
Rayburn stove
Some toads.
A forgotten kitchen out back,
With an ancient old oven,
Stone sinks,
A giant mangle.

The whole house strung together with servants' bells
Linked in the hall
For the long-gone servants to hear.

"This is all ours to play in?
All this?" Alice asked,
Her small arms flung out.
"All of it?"

Outside
A once formal back garden,
Two privies,
A herby old greenhouse,
More toads.
Goose Pie Lane and the farm just
Over the wall,
Shrieking peacocks
Crash landing to terrorise us,
Preferring our lawn to their farm.

A walled kitchen garden,
Gooseberry, currant and raspberry bushes
All overgrown.
Giant artichokes,
Rambling box hedges,
A huge rabbit hutch.
"Can we have a rabbit?"
"No"
"Can we have a puppy?"
"We'll see."
Which meant yes.

An orchard with apple and pear trees for climbing,
And walnut,
Stretching down towards the farthest corner
Where the old rubbish dump for the Rectory had been.
Where the puppy would later dig holes
And the earth turn up inkwells and oyster shells,
Stone bottles for beer,
Glass plates of an early photographer,
Fading fast in our twentieth century sun.
Dad swiftly called the museum who remarkably
Posted back images made from the muddy glass remnants we'd found.

"Do you think this is Reverend Marsh, Dad?"
A gentle faced, curious Victorian
Holding a small accordion
Looked out from his own time

Through his own Rectory window, into ours.

Meanwhile Church Powers had decided that this old Rectory
Had outlived its time,
They would build a new one to replace the old
Our family first in.
They gave us a colour chart
To pick our own paint.

But during that first summer
While the diocesan architects measured and drew

We had free range of

Six acres
Six conker trees
Stables and outbuildings.

Our punt waiting patiently
Among rusty old tools and machinery.
We made dens in these buildings
But more often in trees.
Or the pigsty at the back of the orchard,
Behind the greenhouse,
And in the Rectory itself.

Together or in solitary time,
Then later with friends we made,
We played and gave our minds space.

The freedom of boundless possibility,
Do whatever you like. Play always.
That space in our heads
Never closed.
That summer and for
Years after,
Our minds ran as wild as the garden.

And better that this,
We saw Mum and Dad
Happy together again.
Amused by our ways and in love.
How do children know when parents are happy?
Not by thinking
But by feeling unencumbered
And able to play without worry.

Mum played *Country Gardens* on the piano,
We danced down the French window steps
Onto paving stones trailing sweet jasmine,
Humming with bees,
Barefoot in our nighties,
Breathing fresh
Norfolk air.

I set about curing a fear.
Made a ring of stones,
Then a carefully built a
Small, contained

Bonfire.
Set it,
Lit it, watched it burn,
Poured on water from my small watering can,
Simple procedure,
Over and over.

I set fires all over the garden,
Watering can at the ready.
Ring of stones round.
I would not leave the
Fire
Until it was out.
Stamped right out.

I was in charge of my fires.
They weren't secret.
We didn't need secrets.

"Just look at her"
I heard Dad say to Mum.
"Sound psychology.
"Redeemed from fire by fire".
Whatever that meant,
But I heard the pride in his voice
And I knew they were caring.
They smiled from the kitchen,
Where Alice sat in long conversation
With Mr Bramble.

Alice made many friends of all ages
Mr Bramble was one,
Leant over his spade
As he listened
Punctuating Alice's ramblings with solemn nods.

Mrs Tubby another.
She lived in the bungalow next to the church
And sat out her days in a chair.
"Tubby by name
And by nature,"
Said mum.
"Well, her legs are too heavy to move, Mum."
Explained Alice.

Once I set a fire
In the airing cupboard.
Space and time to do private things
Time to try, time to fail,
We made space for each other.
And so I had space
To learn
All by myself
That it was quite weird
To set fires inside.
And possibly dangerous
And also not necessary.

So I cleared up
And stopped there.
Fires could not catch and consume us
And I wasn't mental like Bill White and Mossie
Was I?
So why be afraid?
And dad was not mental
And mum was not sad
So I stopped.

There was sea only ten miles away.
After half a term settling to school
We had summer holiday.
Being a teacher,
Mum didn't work through the summer

Dad's work was just
Dad being himself,
In and out of his churches,
Up and down the lanes
Between churches.
Four besides Cawston.
Old names of old villages
Old English, Saxon and Viking

Haveringland had a
Saxon round tower
Growing up from a hay field
Lonely beacon of

Early Christians
Spooky Booton,
Sometimes Saxthorpe and Corpusty,
In interregnum.
Dad needed that scooter.
On hot days
Bare legs stuck to plastic seats,
We drove to the sea with some friends and a Mum,
Who was Mum's old best friend.
Jackie and Paula,
Alice and Jess,
Gloria and Mum
Off to the beach.
Gloria had trained as a singer,
Back in the days when our mums were music students.
She led ghoulish lyrics:
Oh mother come quick for I feel very sick and I wanna lie down and die.
And jingles from adverts:
If you want a lot of chocolate on your biscuit join our club.

"Sun, sky and sea kiddoes"
Said Gar when she came on the bus.
"And garden, Gar!"
"Yes, such a garden."
"And a puppy Gar!"
"Even a puppy,
So lucky."

Gar came often on the
National Express
And at Easter with Grandpapa
In the Dormobile,
Parked in our drive.

A boy appeared.
Bright, round faced and cheery,
With flame-coloured hair.
He appeared on his bike at the top of the drive.
"Hello. Mum's polishing poos in the church" he said, grinning
so wide and so easy.
He made me laugh with his joke Norfolk accent.
"We make our own beeswax for polish.
My name's Alastair.
Will you come round?
I've got rabbits."

Dad was repairing the punt in the outhouse,
Preparing for sale.
Painstakingly rubbing down,
Varnishing.
I tried to help,
Sandpapered my hands.
"Why are we selling our punt, Dad?"
"It's time to go sailing" he said.

One day in the outhouse
A new boat appeared

In place of the punt.
Small and boat shaped,
Like a child's drawing.
With white furled up sails.
"She's called Ivory,
Isn't she lovely?

A Gull,
From the south coast of England.
She should sail well on the Broads."
"And the sea, Dad?"
"Yes, maybe."
"The angel has brought you a boat,
Like your dream."
"So he has."
"Is an angel a 'he' Dad?"
Asked Alice.
"It's not always easy to tell."

Voice

In these days
Music hung on the wind,
Taken for granted.
I did perfunctory piano
Didn't progress
In much the same way I did gym club or swimming.
Talent-freely.
We picked out the tunes that we needed
By ear
And we didn't learn to read music,
Though both pretended
And hoped no one noticed.

Then a cello appeared when I was eleven
And Dad brought home
In a little black box
A silver cornet
For Alice.
They weren't pushy parents,
"You could learn if you like?"
"Okay, thanks."

In the lead up to Easter
I hurtled to church my usual way,
As though it was our own.
In my grubby dungarees

And my wellies,
Just looking for Dad,
To say supper was ready.
I pushed open the side door

Let the bright seraphim in burning row
Their loud uplifted angel trumpets blow

Trumpet fire,
And over the trumpet,
A boy.
Loud, uplifted
And soaring
And burning
And piercing
My heart.

"Slower for
Cherubic host!"
Called Dad from the back, to our organist.
"Give Kevin time to breathe."
Our lovely organist slowed pace
Obediently.

Let the cherubic host
In tuneful choirs
Touch their immortal hearts
with golden wires.

I perched on a pew,
Needing more time to breathe
No words
For this state
Only colours
And the colours were fire.

"Hello darling.
How are you?
What do you think?" Dad asked me.

The treble,
The trumpet,
Loud uplifted.
I had risen to be with the angels.

Our hammer beam angels
Watched and heard from the roof.
Those angels that Dad had with a smile,
Called life-size.

"He's good, Kevin, isn't he?
What do you think?" Dad asked me again.
"This will be his last year.
His voice must break soon.
He has that bloom, you know,
That a treble has just before..."

Just before what?
There goes Dad again,
Talking to me like I know
And about a boy's singing,
Never noticing mine.

But I knew
What Dad meant about Kevin
And everything else
In a brilliant minute.
Agape
Counterpoint
Deep conversations
Which largely went over our heads
While we played, careless for years
In the garden
And fields beyond
Now all made sense.
This was love.

"This is Handel," Dad said.
"Like Harmonious Blacksmith, Dad?"
"The same."
Not the same at all.

"Slower for this section, Sylvia!"
Dad boomed.
She was no Simon Preston.
Sylvia had cataracts.

This piece might be hard for her.
So many celestial notes
From an ancient,
Noncompliant organ.
I clutched at a
Beetle eaten pew end,
To steady me.
Awkward to have suddenly found
God,
Love and music
And with Dad so nearby.

I brushed tears from my scruffy outdoors face
Rubbed my tears on my anorak.
Music brought me up short.
Found me wanting.

Light streamed from the loftiest windows,
Lit the cherubic host.

"Touch their immortal hearts with golden wires"

Sang Kevin
Impossibly beautifully.

Golden wires,
Stretch from us to the
Immortal hearts of those
Gone Before.

Instant love fierce as fire
For the slight, unassuming boy
Who could sing this way,
Who could tear at your immortal heart,
Stop your throat,
Beautiful as a rose,
Rising up through the nave.

I was like Mother Julian
Having a vision, quite possibly.

"It's harps," said Dad.
"What?"
Dad was smiling,
Moving backwards,
Cupping his hand to his ear.
"You said hearts Jess. It's *harps*."

Did Dad guess that I had found
God and Love in one beat?
"Perhaps Graham behind Kevin for balance," he said
In front of the rood screen.
"What do you think?"

"Harps Dad, *harps*?"
"Yes, Jess."
"*Harps* with golden wires?"
"Immortal harps, yes."
"Oh"
Immortal harps less satisfactory

And quite soppy
Actually.

I looked up at the strong Cawston angels,
Keeping watch over six hundred years.
Immortal meant living forever
Like the angels,
Like those
Gone Before.

"They haven't got harps, Dad."
"Hmm?
No, not these ones.
Or maybe just that one, look carefully."
"They haven't got trumpets either."
Were there angels other than hammer beam?

I knew it was good to have
Hammer beam angels.
I knew Dad was so proud to show
Pilgrims who trekked from all over
To see.

"These are full length seraphim."
Dad said to me now.
"This piece is called
Let the Bright Seraphim,
For our Pascal Candle Service
Do you like it?"

I could only nod
And grin back at Dad.
A new portal had opened,
I knew what Love was
In its highest form.

Before Saturday
We had our Pascal candle to make in a drainpipe,
Melting down last year's in a saucepan.
We had our church to fill with daffodils
And beeswax polish and
Gar and Grandfather.
This was what happened at Easter.
Our Cawston tradition.

I had sudden knowledge
Of world's end and beginning
A moment of all understanding,
Passing all understanding,
Like they say it is for a drowning man.

"This should wake them up a bit."
Said Dad, striding back up the aisle.

"I came in to say supper is"

"Graham, Kevin, Sylvia Thank you all
That sounded great.
Thanks so much."

Dad was rubbing his hands
In exuberance mixed with anxiety
Always his way.

Sitting at the back,
Running fingers over holey pew-ends,
I longed for dad to say
"One more run through",
To hear once again
And be lost again
To the fire of love.

But everyone had to get home
For their tea.
Kevin was packing his music case
Under the rood screen,
Blinking at Dad.
He listened respectfully,
With the air of a fellow musician.
I was a kid in an anorak
Who had only just heard the bright seraphim.

Graham, Sylvia and Kevin came down the aisle.
"Need a lift home to Sygate, Kev?"
"No thanks, Got my bike."
They all smiled at me,
A child in my pew.

"Hello Jessica"
Said Kevin
Oddly formal.
No one called me my whole name.
He was being polite.
"Did that sound alright?"
"Hello Kevin.
Yes it did."
I wished for musical words to insert,
I was just a beginner,
Had just picked up my cello.
And wasn't allowed in the choir.

The choir was linked to
A boys' school
Up the road,
Just another boys' only choir
Mumbling ones mostly,
Who stared at their feet,
Not electric at all.
'The Silent Witness'
Mum called them.
But Kevin was part of that choir.

I felt unaccomplished.
I had spent too many years
In the garden and fields beyond
With the dog.

"That's high." said Kevin, now looking kindly at me.
"Up to top A
My voice is breaking."

I nodded,
All nonchalant.
Glanced up at the bright seraphim
Who gave nothing away.
Kevin's singing had brought them alive
Now they looked back, blank and wooden.
His voice was not broken
But heavenly.
A heart-breaking rose
In late bloom.

"Well, see you, then, Jessica."
"Yeah, bye Kevin."

Dad called a thank you to Kevin,
Goodbye to Sylvia and Graham
And I padded after him
Around the church.
As we did
As he tidied up
Carefully.
Dad felt under the organ bench for the key
Snapped the shutters shut over keyboard
And locked it.

"Why lock the keyboard?"
"We call it the console."
"Do we?"

"This organ is delicate and Early,
We don't want just anyone having a go"
Dad said briskly, then half to himself
"Kevin has lessons with Sylvia,
But is doing so well, he might need a new teacher."

"Could Ally or I play the organ, Dad?"
"You're too young.
And you haven't progressed much with piano,
Have you?"
"Mrs Tapping's old
And quite mean."
"Is she?"
Dad looked alarmed and alert.
He would not have people be harsh to us.
Piano lessons made my hands hot and lumpy.
Mrs Tapping taught all us village kids,
In her airless bungalow on Back Lane.
Using Ezra Reid Tutor
Which Mum said was
Rather old fashioned.
We yawned through my lessons.
Often we gave up and just watched the tennis together,
On her loud colour telly
Mrs Tapping and me.

Now, I wanted to soar on the organ,
Sing like Kevin.
To matter to Dad in musical ways.
Stuff Mrs Tapping.
"She's not really mean Dad,
Just dreary."
Dad chuckled at my attempt to impress with an adjective.
We said goodnight to God and
The angels,
Left through the chancel side door.

We crunched home together
Over new deep gravel.

"Dad, could you and mum start a choir
That we could all be in?
A village choir?"

"Strange you should say that,
Mum and I have been talking,
We have a plan."
Dad looked directly down at me
For an unusual moment.

"You'd like that, wouldn't you, Jess?
It's time you were singing."
"I'd love it, Dad!
So would Alice!

Not just boys then?"
"No not just boys.
The college choir master is retiring.
Cawston is great but it's no Cathedral.
Boys-only choirs are wasteful
When we have you both and your friends."
Yes, at last!

"Their loud uplifted
a-a-a-angel
tru-umpets blow"
I hummed just loud enough for Dad to hear
As I kicked off my wellies,
Ran upstairs to tell Alice
The Good News
Missing out that I was in love.

Consort

Choir began just after Easter
And as on that day when
We first passed the Pineapple,
Our little world shifted.

Music had been near,
But hadn't involved us before.
Now our parents were
Persuading people of all persuasions
Into our choir.
An eclectic mix.

A gentle shy Brandiston baritone.
A Rolls Royce engineer from Howard's Way.
A dashing accountant from Stocks Loke who
Sang tenor,
And tidied Dad's tax
And played squash with Mum.
Roger and Stephen and
Their little sister, Jo,
All much older and wiser.
Alice's happy gaggle,
My friends, more self – conscious
But keen.
The late teens, early twenties
The Aucklands, Barkhams, Boags, Brownsells
Cooks, Carters, Farnhams,

Frys, Keys, Nunns,Norgroves,
Risboroughs, Selwyns
Tubbys, Tuddenhams,
Wabys,
All who could sing
And some who could not.
Not Alastair because he was away
At his boarding school.
But his sister who went to my school
And was older and clever and musical
And understood all things.
Or so it seemed to me.

We rehearsed in the church
And when church was too cold,
In the Rectory.
Alice and I came alive
To our parents' ability
To work as a musical team.
Music had brought them together
Far back in the sixties.
Not the Beatles and
Summer of love,
But Parry and Purcell,
Wesley and Walton
In St John's Wood Choir
And Trinity College,
Where it seemed
All their friends had paired off in similar ways

And married each other.

We learnt simple anthems
With difficulty.
Mum taught us the notes,
Dad interpretation.
Both matter in music.

Lead me Lord, Wesley progressing to
Mozart's *Ave Verum.*
"Standard fare" said Mum, smiling at Dad
As we craned and crooned up for
In cruce
Settling down to our own kind of harmony
Pro homine
"Authentic" laughed Dad.

One Thursday in May
God ascended.
To mark this event our choir
Climbed up onto the roof
And sang from the precipitous roof-top
And over the village and over the fields
For miles and miles
Hail the Day that sees Him Rise,
Alleluia!
Some villagers complained that we disturbed the peace.
We didn't mind.

Years

There had never been
Reason to doubt that
God was a loving,
If absent-minded father,
His greatest gifts
Music and love.
But in Cawston we lived in the moment,
We had played
Without care,
Had been careless for years.

Well, thank God for choir, because
Now change
Marched in.
I tried to write
All of it down
As Mr Kett had primed us to do.
School alarmed me
Increasingly.
Mr Kett's ways were replaced
In my new
Norwich school
By formidable women.
I got out of my depth fast and frighteningly,
Try

Writing that

Down,

Village girl!

Quite impossible.
Help!

If you can't find the words
To express yourself
Put a cheery face on
School life at home
And hope they won't notice
And live for
Choir practice
And the ever expanding
Imagery of
Hymnody.

Being cheery was what naturalists might call
An adaptation.
Reverend Theodore Henry Marsh might talk this way
About plants
In Victorian times.
Modern psychologists might think differently.

And then Dad got ill
So the ground was unsure
All that Autumn.

Fragmenting.
Mum strung out
Dad absent.
In hospital then convalescing.
"What is wrong with Dad?"
"No one quite knows, darling."
They said diabetes and gave him a diet sheet
Which he ignored.
Choir limped on.

Advent came.
While rehearsing
Gabriel's Message
For our Carol service
Dad had a hypo.
Slower and slower
He made us sing over and over

The Angel Gabriel from heaven came

"Slower, you're rushing!"

His wings as drifted snow

"No, more slowly, much slower
You rush!
You are speeding, rush rushing
Oh can you not hear?
Can you not hear the angels?"

Our choir was bemused.
Had the rector gone mental?
We all watched Dad anxiously
Trying to follow his wandering beat.

His eyes aflame

We petered out
All eyes on Dad,
Who was crouched,
Head in hands
At the foot of the altar,
Weeping.

Was Gabriel up there in the roof
Eyes aflame?
Where were the seraphim on this occasion?
Or was it all just dead wood
And dead icons.

The kind, gentle men of our choir
Took Dad home
And we trailed behind.
Embarrassed
And not understanding.

Mum's face was all worry.
"I'm sorry,
I'm becoming a burden."

"It isn't your fault Dad"
Said Alice, slipping her hand in his.
"It's your diabetes."

We pulled together for the Carol Service,
Dad mustering all his blood sugar
To project
The length of the church
Bidding us to prayer
from the back of the Nave.

"We remember those
Who rejoice with us
Upon another shore
And in a greater life,
Whose hope
Is in the word made flesh."

Kevin recorded the service
And afterwards
After everything
We played the tape over and over.
The way Dad's voice cracked on 'hope',

We heard his hope, expectation.
And then,
Since he was right by the microphone
His bass bawling out through each carol
To steady the basses.
"Come thou long expected Jesus"

His expectation,
Israel's hope,
Dad's sure and certain
Hope in it all.

"Choir's got really good" said red-haired Alastair after.
"I wish I could be in the choir."

Leap forward
To Easter,

"Quite yet?"
Says robin,
Who I had forgotten
But who rests on the wall,
Sceptical, breast aflame.

"Christmas being more my season, after all.
And you with more to relate."

Yes.
Straight on
To our last Easter
In Cawston.
Two years since my seraphic moment
When music rolled in on the tide.
I could play Handel now,
My favourite, a lyrical song in D major,
Not stretching

Have you seen my lady
A walking in the garden.

"Lovely tone, Jess"
Dad would say.
So I'd play it again.

And Alice got so good
On her small silver cornet
That they bought her a trumpet
And she opened Easter.

A small girl
Alone
The font step her podium,
A false start,
"Oh bother."
Then a faultless performance,
Brave,
Loud, uplifted.
Foretelling how Alice would go.

Did Dad see her potential,
Know that Alice would go on
To make music her life,
Conducting
All over the world?

That Easter Saturday
Purposeful flower ladies set about church,
Mum among them.
Daffodils stood in
Buckets of water
The lilies rolled in
From the florist in Aylsham,
Parishioners bought them
In Loving Memory of relatives whose work was done.
Making ready.
Beeswax buff to old oak,
Sweeping cool stone,
Light stone morning
Kevin practising the organ,
His voice having broken
And Sylvia off for her cataracts op.

Chi Rho
"The initials of Christ, do you see?" Dad explained.
"In Greek, Dad?"
"Yes, that's right."
Painted painstakingly onto the candle
In real gold leaf.
Made new from the drainpipe,
By Dad who was stronger
If not quite restored
To himself.

I had adjusted to Love and the Universe
Admirably, I felt.

Channelling love for the boy
Into various loves;
My cello
My new bicycle.
Where might that take me?
Over to Sygate to see Kevin quite often,
I hoped.

A cobalt blue Raleigh.
Thank you Gar
Thank you Grandpapa,
Thank you so much!
"Tha's bootiful", nodded Gar, doing Norfolk.
"You're only thirteen once, darling girl."
"Don't worship your bicycle as some do their cars",
Warned Grandfather
In his church voice.

I worshipped my bike in the beauty of holiness.
Kevin too
And music.
I may have mistaken
Music for God.
Or God for music

Medias Via
The middle of things.
Start in the middle.

"No, start as you mean to go on".
Says the robin, so bossy.

Beginning and middle and end
Will be here, in this midwinter churchyard
Our time, our parents time,
Dead and alive.
All time today.

"What of the angel?" he asks me.
"The stranger who led your father,
Who brought you to Cawston?"

The dream was a portent of what was to come and to bring us around
To the here and the now and the always.

"Your story is unfinished.
A robin can be more reliable
As guide
Than an angel.
Just saying" he sings.

I want to stay here with my story,
Family led to a life more lovely
By a dream vision.

The robin gives his sideways stare,
Piercing.

"But that is not all."

"Are you robin or angel?
Watcher or messenger?
Stranger or friend?"
There need be no more than
Mr Kett and the cherishing school,
Village life in its humdrum appeal,
Fields and garden
Parents and children,
Awakening of love through new musical sounds.
"Are you a robin or an angel?"

"I am what you need to believe."

"Whoever heard of a
robin of death?
An angel of death,
But a robin?"

"But a robin has fire in his breast."

Ring his knell

"No."

My heart hurts for that family,
Unbearably.
What happened is history,
Can we not keep them safe in the
Shadow of Cawston,

Those yesterday's children
And the next bit not happen?
Golden wires between us
Holding immortal hearts
Reaching up, stretching down
Holding immortal hearts
Immortal harp strings?
There is such love
Among the angels.
All shall be well.
Why tell more?

"Go there again"
Says the messenger

Deranged
When a robin
Sings my poem
From the bough of a yew tree.

"You need big poetry for this story,
Not your wandering mediocre musings alone.
One day in the garden
The church and the daffodils
Next, in the sea and the lilies.
You faced down death,
You, your little sister and those children
From the apple tree.
You faced down death.

And a robin has fire in his breast."

Yes.

Nothing of him that doth fade

"I am the only colour in the churchyard today.
And the colour is crimson for blood that was shed".

Yes.

Back, then.
Very well.
Back.

At Sea

Sleeping bag girl
Safe from the world
In a nylon bag
In a nylon tent
Hang onto your sanity
Sleeping bag girl.

One reason to sleep in the tent tonight
Is so as not to run into Dad on the landing.
He died today
But may not have yet realised.
Are they told?
He had no time for convention
I fear he may break taboos,
Wander out of Heaven's Bounds,
Especially at this early stage.
Does an angel guard or guide them?

The Lord should look out for Dad
Since he was a loyal friend.
But then there is Teresa of Avila, also dead;
"If God treats his friends this way,
Is it any wonder he has so few!"

I can see Dad tickled by the joke,
Laughing and scratching,

Exuberance making his eczema worse.
When someone has died you will not
Hear them laugh again out loud.
Simple enough.
They are unlikely to come back unless they are
Jesus.
Calm the storm,
Walk on the water.
Rise again.

After the storm the weather is cooler,
But Rebecca and I are quite warm
Just here
In our nylon sleeping bags,
Canvas batting softly against the guy ropes,
Smell of old mould and duck water.

I may go back to my bedroom tomorrow,
But tonight I will stay here in the garden,
In my childhood tent
Write my diary in the usual way.
This is something I can decide on.
Mum understands.

Alice is safe in her yellow-blue room
Under the eaves.
Colours she chose for this bedroom
From the Dulux range
The diocese provided;

Delphinium and Mimosa;
Two walls in each carefree colour.

My dad and Tim had chosen estuary
Over the Broads.
Hickling Broad would have been fine for a
Gentler adventure.
A gentle lake with
Miss Turner Island
Safe in the middle,
Among reeds and marsh gas.

Grand scale adventure,
Such as we had today,
Would never be good.

When he needed peace
From the parish
And from his own mind,
Dad would sail out to Miss Turner Island
And stay nights away
In this tent of ours.

Dad checked Conditions with the coastguard
This morning, before we left.
Over Easter we had a freak heat wave,
"But this sort of weather can't last"
Dad had said.
He was careful,

Not a risk-taking man
As people may have thought,
Though accidents did seem to happen.
Risk took advantage of him.

There will be an inquest,
They will ask why he wore no life jacket.

Dad has not been well lately.
It is not just his age,
Which is forty.
Mum deals with things,
Looks after all of us.
I have not asked.

And now cannot ask.
Everything Alice and I wonder about him
Will be answered in a posthumous light now
By people who are not Dad.
I would rather have stayed in the garden.

We tacked up the estuary slowly,
Packed into our boat;
Tim, Dad, Richard,
Rebecca, Paulus,
Alice and me.

A Gull
Is an uncommon sight

In Norfolk,
Small with pretty hull,
Curving into the wave and the wind.
A soft curve to the white mainsail.
Dad says the Gull is more often sailed
In the South.

Scolt Head Island,
Shelduck and Wader,
Widgeon and Teal,
Curlew and Brent Goose and Pink Footed Goose,
Sandwich Turn
Little Turn.
Richard recited the litany
Of birds we might see
On the island or estuary.

When we reached the peninsular
That at high tide turns into an island,
Someone suggested a sea sail.
While Paulus and Alice played
High in the dunes.
As we drew out,
We watched them leaping in
Snowy soft sand.

Tim stayed to look after them,
Gathered driftwood for a fire,
Readying for our return.

I have mixed feelings for sailing,
Dad may have known.
Alice is a natural.
She took to sailing
When we first went on the Broads.
I always preferred to stay home in the garden.

"When we say 'Ready about', Dad',
Can the wind hear us?" she had asked.
"How does the wind know to change?"
Alice had curiosity,
Alice loved sailing.
I knew about tacking from
Swallows and Amazons.
I had a wistful idea of a sailor girl
But she never was me.
Rebecca was going along with her family consensus, maybe,
And Richard had wild birds to see.

The rudder broke,
Our first hitch.
In the estuary mouth
A strange new wind got up.
We jibed and the rudder snapped off.
Dad leant over the stern in his jeans
And his rusty red fisherman's top
That he always wears.
What he never wore was a lifejacket,
"It gets in the way

When you are sailing."
But might of course be useful
If you were drowning.

I was up in the bows
Where usually I feel safe.
But we were drifting to
Larger and larger waves.

The sun had gone in,
The sky dark against heavy grey sea,
Those voices, the sea voices.
The waves were too big.
Rebecca said she felt cold.
Dad and Richard did not seem to hear her.
They were busy with our broken rudder.

One thing happened, then another.

A reasonable time was replaced
With a terrible time,
But that is in keeping
With my experience
Of sailing.

Water came in.
"White water is fine
Only worry if green water comes into your vessel"
Dad used to explain.

Green water came in.
Then a great wave,
Bigger than everything
Rose up to our right,
I mean starboard,
And we were thrown in.

We heard Dad call;
"Hold onto the hull!"
I had bobbed up in my life jacket.
Dad always made *us* wear them.
Good father.
He was a good father.

Freezing water was stealing my breath,
But I heard him call.
We all held on to the edge.
I saw Richard and Rebecca grip tight on the port side,
Dad climbing onto the hull, tugging.
Three times we tried pulling her up.
We knew capsize drill,
We tried to help,
But the waves were deafening,
Defeating.

Use words like 'defeating'
And it feels like a battle.
Fear is
Greater than the waves,

Because this is a fight you can't win.

I felt sleepy.
I felt like not bothering to win.
I had edged round to the rudderless stern
And thought I would rest, holding on there.
I thought;
"This will do."

But Richard had dragged himself
Into the boat
And was hauling his sister on board.
Rebecca was light but made heavy
With soaking wet clothes.
He pulled her, with boys' strength.
How useful to have a big brother
To pull you, with boys' strength
I thought.

I wanted to mention the great wave to Dad.
We had no big brother,
But we had a Dad who would talk about boys' stuff,
Sizeable waves that surprise you,
Rudders that snap
And so on.
So sleepy
My life blood sugar may be ebbing
Out with the tide.
Never mind.

"Come on Jess, try!"
So I tried
Because it was not so hard
To pull myself up,
Even having girl's arms
And dredged energy from somewhere.
Richard helped.
And only when I was back,
Propped up in the waterlogged hull,
Noticing that both my wellies and socks were gone,
Did I fully wake up.

Then I wanted to win that battle again
And I looked around for Dad.
We were thrown,
Side to side
On the slippery wet wood.
We heard Dad shout;
"Pull the mast out!
The sail is dragging her back over!"

We understood,
Moved to the bows,
Pulled
All of us,
Until the mast came away.
I looked out before we threw sail and mast
Of Dad's pride and joy
Back into the sea.

Would it be alright to just
Chuck the sail overboard?

I couldn't see Dad to ask.
I couldn't see much at all,
Beyond spray and unfathomable grey.
Do you understand that I could not see
Or move, help,
Jump in, save,
Think
Even?

We sat, waist deep in water, waiting.
They have told us we waited an hour and a half.
Tim, Alice and Paulus
Were tiny small specks on the coastline.
We could see shore,
But surrounding us
Sea and more sea.

We were drifting west,
Towards The Wash
And I wondered
How far might a boat drift?
Is westward better than Northerly?
Where is the next piece of land?

"Where is the lifeboat?"
Rebecca was crying.

Well you would.
I was not sure lifeboats came out
This far from a harbour.
I could see why she might be upset.

We felt cold to our bones
Until we could not feel,
Except in our small, warm mouths.

Awkwardly
We sang hymns to lift our spirits
In this dreadful adventure.
Not
"Eternal Father Strong To Save"
That was too close to home.
But carols, with descants like
"Once in Royal."

Richard's voice croaky
Like Kevin's is now.
No seraphic melody
No angels in sight
Or were they hovering?
Where was Dad's messenger
Dream angel
Readying to pull us to shore?
Gone to Dad?
I hoped he had angels about him.

I thought of the Rectory and garden
And wanted so much to be back
Playing cricket with borrowed brothers
From our friends' families
As we were yesterday.
Were we yesterday's children already?

It was supposed to be choir practice tonight
Taken by Dad.
I love choir.
And Dad.

There was no rope to throw
And we could not see him.
He had gone.
That was just how things were.

A story might start here,
Begin like this.
A film might start this way.
Or end.
But when real drama happens events look unspectacular,
Awkward.
Or is it that being thirteen,
Everything awkward already?

Richard wanted to swim for the shore.
We would not let him.
He is a boy,

A soon to be adult boy.
He needed to be strong to save.

Richard lives to watch birds.
Sometimes he pointed out
Some grey old bird,
As we sat freezing to death.

"I suppose that's an albatross, Richard?"
"Wrong hemisphere, Jess."

He mustered a grin.
We have squatted together
In bird hives along this coast,
Me missing the point
Of ornithology,
Eyes glazing over,
Longing for home.

"Birds are important" the robin reminds me.
"I know that now."

Later they told us we
Saved Richard's life by not letting him swim,
As he did ours by dragging us back on the boat

Before we drifted away.

No one saved Dad.

When the lifeboat sped
Out of the estuary
We were not dead
Or waiting to die,
But back to life
And the rest of it.
I heard Richard say:
"I love you, Jess."
I expect that was relief.

Our boat was our island.
Still, without sail
Transferring to lifeboat was tricky,
We had to destabilise,
I could see fear in
The lifeboat man's face.
Even he was afraid of the sea.
Brave, big and
Ready to rescue us
With hard warm calloused hands,
He helped us across one by one,
His face tight, concentrating.

A younger man, maybe his son
Silently stood at the tiller.
Their faces suggested
We might still die,
All of us.
And them.

"All of you?"
We stared at him.
Dumb.

"Is this all of you?"
"My Dad was with us" I said.
"I think he got swept away."

He nodded, looked quickly about him.
We all looked.
Of course we couldn't see Dad,
But we looked,
As though he might appear,
Beckon us over to collect him next,
As though he were waiting
Just at the next bus stop.

"Come on,
Let's get you back.
Hold tight to the ropes."
We sped in.
The sea smacked at the mouth of the estuary,
White water foamed over us.
No green.
We flew over the waves,
Bouncing hard down each time.
Richard silent
I never know what he is thinking.
I know so few boys.

Rebecca was crying.
"We'll pick up the little 'uns now"
Said the lifeboat man.
"They were left on the island
With bird watchers,
When your Dad ran for help,"
He explained, with a man's nod to Richard.

My little Alice
Their little Paulus
So small.
Nine is not always so small,
But young for a day like today.
Their faces were white as we raced up to them,
Both shrank back as cold water poured over their wellies.
Alice looked around, puzzled.
"Where's Daddy?"

I felt ashamed to have gone out
With a Dad and returned
Without one.

Alice looked little, white, worried.
"We don't know." I said.
"My Daddy…"
She started to cry.
She had not said goodbye
Nor had I.
"Ssh" said the lifeboat man,

Needing to concentrate.
"Let's get you all back."

No-one spoke after that
And when we reached the staithe
Silent people stood on the quay,
Staring.
We could not feel our feet on the flints.

We trailed up to the lifeboat house,
After our saviour.
I tried to look normal
And every-day,
Wondering how often the lifeboat man
Had rescued children
And cared for them
Back in his bungalow.
Rebecca and I suddenly in a bathroom
With lilac wall-paper
Richard next door in a shower.
Mr Beck came in with sugary tea.
That was his name. Mr Beck, lifeboat man,
As we sat end to end in
His purple bath.

"Sweet tea. Good for shock."
He held the mugs at arms-length,
Eyes averted.
Rebecca and I giggled.

Was that shock or just a strange man in the bathroom?
He did not stay,
Looked away,
Hurried out to his radio.

The water was tepid
We shivered.
I wanted to pour the hot tea on my skin.
Where was Alice?
Was she okay?
We could hear distant crackling
Radio voice
As we sat in the water.
Through a small, misted-up window
We could see out and over the staithe.
We could hear a huge roar overhead now,
Peering out through the steam we saw
A yellow
Sea King helicopter
Weaving up the creek
Out to sea.

"They're looking for Dad."
Becca nodded
Her face pale green
Like washed seaweed.
My friend Becca.
She had hardly spoken
I felt guilty about her.

We had ruined her holiday.
She didn't mention her own Dad,
But I knew she was waiting to hug him
And hold him
And know he was still real.

Having seen our sail go down three times
Tim had left the children with a couple of twitchers
Hailed a lift in a rowing boat over the estuary.
Then he had run the two miles to the Staithe
To alert the lifeboat.
A long way for a man over forty.

When we were dry and someone had given us
Clean jeans and jumpers
No knickers,
We joined Alice and Paulus
In Mr Beck's steamy conservatory.
We sat in a half circle
Not on the neatly cushioned cane sofas
But up against them on the floor,
Hugging our knees.

We sat for a bit,
Then
Tim came in,
Ducking to fit his tall body
Under the door frame.
Mr Beck the lifeboat man

Stood in the doorway
Short next to Tim
As most people are
And two policemen followed.

All these men were too big for this hot, tidy home.
Becca ran up to Tim and he pulled her close
Then stood her gently aside.
I thought
Here we go.
Tim moved over to us,
Placed his large hands first over my head
Then on Alice's,
Like a bishop in
Blessing.

We stared up at him.
I wanted to smile
To make it easier for him, to say
"Oh never mind"
As if some minor tragedy
Had occurred
Like my bike being stolen.
I love my bike.

Maybe Alice was crying.
Someone was.

"The helicopter found your father.

He's dead."

"Poor Mummy."

Tim's kind eyes were steady on us.

"I am going to ring the Mums now."
Another shit job for Tim, I thought.

"Can we wait in the car Dad?" asked Richard

We sat in their car by the slip way,
Waiting for Tim to finish with people
Like the policemen and men in the
Boatyard.
He seemed to take ages.
We were told that Dad died at eleven o'clock,
By one we were back at the lifeboat man's house.
I think it was round about three
When we began the drive back to our village
So maybe we got home at teatime?
Important to know
Because time drifted by
In the boat
And at some moment
Dad had stopped breathing.

On the drive back to Cawston,
I felt altogether accountable
Returning without Dad

As though we had carelessly mislaid him.

People say 'lost' when they mean died.
Tim had not
Used a euphemism.
They die,
We are lost.

Sick relief that it hadn't been Mum
Then guilty again
About that thought.
In our family we have relied on Mum for most things,
Safe that Dad loves in a less applied way.

Tim drove and I asked him
What he said to Mum.
She had been at the hairdresser.
Penny had answered the telephone,
So had the job of telling Mum when she got home
With her hair done.

"Penny is a doctor, used to breaking bad news."
"Right Dad, but to her oldest friend?" Richard asked.

Tim swung the Volvo round the lanes.
The worn upholstery smelt of old dogs
And damp beach towels.
No one said they felt car sick.
We had one more space than before.

"Penny was concerned for your father."
Tim spoke, serious-eyed, catching ours in the driving mirror.

"She had a long talk with him only last night,
Puzzled why his diabetes was not under control.

Penny had suggested a specialist he might see.
What happened today may have saved him from suffering."
Tim talks straightforwardly, when he talks at all.
He has tufts of grey hair that crinkle up
Off his large, wise head,
Like a Brillo pad.
My father had shiny black hair with no grey.
Different Dads.
Different ways.

As we came round the bend
In the Rectory drive where Dad so often falls off his scooter,
Surprised every time by the deep fresh gravel,
Nine cars were parked.
One of them our London taxi,
Returned yet again from the menders.

Clues as to how we should look lie in others' faces,
Alice at the island,
The staring, strange onlookers,
Tim when he told us,
Now David the tenor.

David's face was death grey.
He was coming away from the Rectory,
Swinging his keys,
Walking towards his Mini Clubman.
He stopped when he heard us crunch up the drive.
Here we were then,
Survivors returning.
No format to follow.
"Your mother is inside with the Bishop."
The Bishop.
Oh God.
This was important then.
Of course, stupid child,
Dad has
Died In Office,
which means, I think,
Not retired.

Alice and I went in,
There was Mum
Sitting next to the Bishop of Norwich.
He has been to our house once before.
We had Schloer when he came as
He doesn't drink wine.
We don't know him so well,
But the Bishop was there at the start
Now this is the end.

"Mum?"
Mum had been crying, but she looked so young and so pretty.
She had just had her hair done, you see.
She is a widow.
Mum kissed us a lot
And said we should know that
Dad was never afraid of dying.
"We know Mum.
We know."

I was frightened
Of dying.
I hadn't wanted to die,
But to be here by the Rectory and Church
And the garden.

"I know"
Says my robin.
"I know."

I had desperately wanted to live
Which we think is the opposite of dying.
But is wanting to live different from
Not being frightened to die?
Dad believed you Live On
But to die,
But to drown in the sea,
He must have been desperately frightened.

"You were sleepy not scared
Before Richard pulled you back on board."

Yes, the robin is right.
I was sleepy just then.
Do angels lull you?
Do angels hover
Waiting to take you home?

My thoughts were so full of the sea,
Was I still dripping water on our carpet in front of the fire?
Mum had her children back,
Her half-drowned children.

Then the bishop, who was not wearing his mitre
But a plain dark suit and pink shirt,
Placed his hands on top of our heads just
As Tim had done.
And then many more people were around
And I am so tired now,
The sequence is hard to remember.

Becca and I had a bath
Hot water this time, still together.
We did not speak much
But I was so glad she was with me.
I sat near the taps, running more and more hot in,
Until the tank was empty.
We played Racing Demon in their caravan,

Parked in our driveway.
Someone spilt milk on the cushions
And no one got cross
Even though stale milk smells forever.

They let us eat supper in front of the telly
And we turned it on to see ourselves
Headline news.
We featured not only on Look East
Which is homespun,
But nationally too.
Our names and ages were wrong.
We were reported as having been rescued
From the North Sea,
Suffering from exposure.

I wonder about suffering and exposure,
About the very ordinariness
Of the extra ordinary,
But I do not have words for these now,
Or a way to express fear
Or love for my family
So I'm staying out here
In the garden.

Drying sails

Tim drove us all back to
Burnham Overy Staithe
The next morning.
Our boat was washed up with the tide.
We will sell our boat back to the boat yard
But wanted our waterproof coats
From the hold.
We stand around the wreck,
Drag out bone dry anoraks.
Dad always extolled the Gull's
Buoyancy system.
His faith, in this regard, rewarded.

The sea has many voices,
Many Gods and many voices.
It tosses up its losses…

"You cannot quote Eliot in your poem."
Says robin fire-breast, primly.

I know,
But he writes about death and the fear
And expresses for me what we cannot express
In perfect sense
Perfect tense
Perfect sentences.

Do you see?

Then we came away,
Having done what people advise;
Revisit the scene,
Get back aboard after a tumble.
People have much to say when such things happen.
Nothing is helpful, but music and poetry.

"Why I sing!"
Soars the robin.

We stopped in Fakenham for Tim to
Buy every newspaper.
He parked in the market square,
Leaving us in the heavy old Volvo together again.
We didn't bicker
We didn't say much.
We felt large amounts of love for each other.
Today, we are gentle together.
Tim came back with copies and threw them all
Into the car.
He does not shield us
Or speak silly words.
The newspapers shout for themselves

"Rector Dies As Freak Wave Hits Dingy."
"Children Saved As Rector Drowns."
In each broadsheet, small copy

All inaccurate in detail.
But what could they say?
This happened in ordinary time.
We read every word,
Then Tim drove us home.

The Rectory is engulfed by a wave
Of arrangements.
Penny will take Becca and Paulus home.
Tim is staying on to help Mum.
Richard says he wants to hang around here.
He mutters something about a bird
That he needs to see

"A robin?"
No my friend, not a robin.

And disappears over the fields with binoculars.

Gar and Grandpapa are coming back,
Having left only on
Easter Monday.
Alice and I had been helping Dad
Make the Pascal Candle
When the grandparents had arrived for Easter.
We had melted creamy beeswax
Down in a pan
And were pouring it into the
Sealed end drainpipe, to set.

The seal had leaked
Just as mum brought them
Into the kitchen with suitcases,
Wax seeping, setting.
A thin film dried over clean lino.
"Hi Gar and Grandpapa, we're just a bit busy!"
"So we see."
We began again,
Scraping wax shaving with kitchen knives
Into the saucepan.
Mum made tea round us.

But this is the kind of incident
Dad was prone to or prey to.
He was trying to save our church's money.
Candles are costly when ecclesiastical.
It may not have improved
Our grandfather's view
Of Dad's liturgical or husbandly ways.
Grandpapa is a different generation
Of husband and clergyman.

The original candle
Which we resurrect every year
Came from Coventry Cathedral
Where Dad was Ordained
Ten whole years ago
When I was three and Alice just born.
Dad is of the modern era,

Honest to God.
Grandpapa,
An Oxford theologian,
Thorough and scholarly
"Though modern too,
For his day,"
Dad would say.

After the candle had set and turned out of the drainpipe
Dad carved the initials of Christ
In gold leaf every year.

"You have said this already."
"I know, bird, but do you see how it was?"

Miniature work for big hands.
Not all in our village are aware of
The Pascal Mystery.
Dad has an uphill struggle with some.

We came to Cawston after Dad's dream
And at the Bishops invitation.
Dad filled the church with
Light, music, theatre,
Charisma.
If they found him eccentric
He did not appear to mind.

Recently, blood sugar made him unstable.
Chaos only held at bay.
Alice and I mind
What people think.
We are part of the village ourselves.

The congregation might not understand.
Did the sea save Dad from more suffering?
Was it not just diabetes, but
Something 'more sinister'?
What?
Did drowning save Dad from a fate worse than death?

Dad's last service was Easter Communion.
Darkness to light
Lilies,
Crystal Sea,
And Love's redeeming work
Being done
As I've mentioned before.
Dad invited Grandpapa to preach
In the church made more lovely by caring and cleaning and love.
Now Grandpapa is back
To help bury Dad.

Our Aunt has arrived.
Mum's sister, Patty.
"Darling girls."
Her hugs are more bony than Mum's.

We help her up the stairs with her case.

"I told a complete stranger on the train, poor man.
The whole tragedy. Poor man."
Is forty so tragically young?
Mum is too young and pretty for widowhood,
But Dad had seemed older.
For him forty might have been right.
Last week I was thirteen,
Childhood left in the sea.
But thirteen is a teenager, time to stop playing anyway.
What about Alice who is only nine?

Patty takes me to Sheringham for my cello lesson.
David the nice accountant tenor drives.
We are trying to keep some normality
In our days.

It is Saturday,
Dad died on Thursday.
Yesterday, our dog bit my arm because
I moved his bowl while he ate,
How stupid.
I know not to do that.

Our kitchen had been full of
People eating
Cadbury's Bournville
Brought round by David, from a chocolate company

Gone into receivership.
"What does receivership mean David?"
"Bankrupt. Unable to function."

People come all day with sausage rolls
To comfort mum, who dislikes sausage rolls.
Mum said Caspar was upset by the atmosphere,
He has gone to kennels for a rest.
I had stitches in Aylsham Cottage Hospital.

Mrs Crow my cello teacher wears
A face of compassion,
"Did you hurt your hand in
"The Accident?"
Adopting a tone.
My arm is restricted by the bandage,
So we stop playing and do some theory.

Afterwards Patty and I head to Woolworths.
"We need sweets."
We fill two large bags with PicknMix
Spending £1.68,
More than anyone has ever spent
On sweets.
We are still laughing about this
When David meets us at the
Sheringham Clock.

In the car
Patty and David discuss
Identification and Inquest.
David had gone to Identify Dad,
Very kind of him.
I am relieved they talk freely,

I look out for churches
Over the wheat green April fields.
You can pick out three towers against the skyline at any time.
I suck more sweets,
The toffee tastes plastic.
I make a noise that isn't laughter.
Patty turns;
"Jess?"
I am almost proud to find myself crying
For a minute I feel like a warm, normal girl
Who is missing her Dad.
Patty climbs into the back to hug me.
"We loved him, Jess. He was wonderful, you know that, don't
you?"
I nod and snivel,
Wipe my nose on my PicknMix bag.
"Want another one?"

Soon we come back into Cawston through Sygate,
Up the bare High Street where nothing much happens,
Except Kevin's Dad's shop.
Past our huge rock of a church.

Cawston was built on the wealth of the wool trade,
Mr Kett taught us.
Money made this great building,
Money and Church and the people.
Money made the rood screen and hammerbeam angels.
No steeple.
Is Dad with the angels now?
And where will our money come from
Now we won't have Church?

Alice went back to school today.
Dad died on Thursday, now it is Monday.
Patty, Richard and I walked her up the school drive
Like bodyguards.
She worries she will get told off
For missing a day to go sailing.
The school flag flies half-mast.
No one will mention the day off.
Her strong little self will be
Reunited with Debbie and Cathy, her friends.
I hope she's okay.

My school starts next week.
Thank God not this.
To pass time, I teach myself violin
In small bursts
That don't hurt my hand.
I practice in Dad's study.
The days since Dad died have seemed long and unusual.

Mum is so busy.
The telephone rings all the time and
I avoid answering.

People are coming from all over the country to the funeral.
Family and friends from all over and people we never met.
Dad liked adults and their muddles,
Also older teenagers.
Some priests concentrate all their efforts on children,
Saying they are the future,
That we should attract them to church,
By making church easy.

But church is not easy.
Dad tended to focus on
The middle aged
Who are trying their best to bring up
Their children, stuck in their marriages,
Maybe despondent at how life is going.

"A couple should not stay together for the sake of the children."
"Shouldn't they, Dad?"
"Life is not always easy. Church should be there. We should be
there for people,
Do you see?"

I have learnt fingering for first position.
Patty comes in sometimes, to help.
Dad's study smells of Dad.

His pipes are everywhere.
The broken demi-john he cut his thumb on last week
Is still under the desk.
So is his blood, in large deep, set drops
On the floor and the door handle.

Dad was working late, preparing for Easter
When he dropped his pen and reaching down for it
Sliced through his thumb
On the jagged lip of the broken jar
He had been saving for
Homemade wine.
Then he had lumbered around the study
Bleeding
Looking for something to
Stem the flow.

His intention had been to minimise fuss for Mum,
Just before Easter, with the grandparents staying
But there was far more bother
When he fainted,
As blood sugar ebbed out of him.
Mum had to drive him to Norwich hospital at midnight,
They stitched up his thumb.
We forgot about the dried blood
That is now dead man's blood.
A relic.
His books line the shelves and cover the desk
And the floor.

Greek, Chinese, Hebrew,
Dad was learning Hebrew from
A rabbi in Norwich and
Chinese from the lady at the
Aylsham Chinese takeaway.
Being dyslexic he preferred to translate
The Gospel from Greek,
Rather than reading the English.
"Jess, how do you spell Rectory?"
Then, further down the same page;
"Darling, how did we spell
Rectory?"

Although I can spell Rectory I have disappointed
With Greek.
Dad tried to teach me from
Wenham's New Testament Guide.
Luo, I lose
Lambano, I take.
"Take a lamb from a barn, such a simple mnemonic."

He is laughing here, in his study now,
Just out of earshot.
Tapping out a pipe or reaching for another cigarette.
Smoking forty fags a day will not have helped
His lungs in the water.
Alice and I fetch him twenty
Lambert and Butler
From the post office.

Fifty pence.
Alice will be good at Greek, being clever
And Dad will never know.
She will need him and he won't be here.

Richard comes in.
He knocks first, which is odd.
"You okay?" I say
We haven't talked much this week.
What can we say?
But I like him around,
Binoculars round his neck,
Stalks of dry grass in his shiny brown hair.
"Yeah. I walked to the clay pits,
Saw a Buff Breasted Sandpiper."
His voice flat.
"But that's good, isn't it?
You've been waiting to spot one of them."
"Meant nothing."
He rubs at the floor with his trainer.
"Jess, is this dried blood?"
Richard doesn't wait for an answer but is off again.
Funny boy.

All Dad's projects scatter this room,
And his mess.
Also porn mags.
Confiscated last week from some boys
At the college.

He had started to burn them outside,
But forgot this batch,
When distracted by something more interesting.
When the Bishop arrived to bless our heads,
I saw single singed breasts blowing in the garden.
And our cess pit has overflowed.

Mum cannot sleep, but she says Tim is always first down in the kitchen
However early she wakes.
Tim sorts and fixes.
He walks first
I see him from my bedroom window, setting off
Over fields and returning, determined.
I will throw the porn mags away soon.
But I might read them first.

The house is quiet this evening.
They are at a requiem mass for Dad,
So his coffin is there, in his church
While the angels keep guard.
Alice and I will both sing in the choir for the funeral.
People say it is better to
Have a role
But of course we will sing.

I ran into church earlier, to pick up my hymn book,
I had forgotten the coffin.
It lay in the aisle like a long, tall person.

I hedged down the south transept
And up into the chancel
To grab my book.
Then I stayed for a bit.
No one else there,
No music.
I had not said goodbye
Or that I loved him.
You can do that to corpses.

Dad and Mum made our choir together.
We took completely for granted that this was their way.
We sing 'manageable anthems'
By Henry Purcell and
Christopher Tye.
The effect is not polished.
Mum will take choir tonight.
How brave, people say.
How stupid people are.
What music can we make now?
Dad told me there are some beautiful
Funeral Sentences
By Henry Purcell.
I doubt we can learn them in time.
They may be
Too ambitious
For Thursday.

I wish he had told me more about music
Which I do understand
And less about Greek
Which I never will.
This clever, so musical man
Who they say was
Unworldly
And who now lies dead
In a long, tall box.
Angels standing guard,
Dry as dust in their sorrow.

"Bye Dad, then.
See you tomorrow."
I felt awkward with only the
Hammer beam angels to hear me,
So left quickly,
Ran back fast through the gate to our Rectory
And back up our drive.

"You okay, darling?"
"I forgot the coffin was there."
Mum hugged me,
The well-wishers
Looked on so knowingly.
They don't know anything actually
So they can fuck off.
It was just a coffin
He wasn't there

No big deal.

"It's okay Mum.
Can I have a biscuit?"
I leant over a well-wisher, to grab a biscuit.
"I'll be in Dad's study."

So the study is where I am.
We never came in much, before
But I like spending time in his space,
Dad's desk looks up the drive
To the Church
So that he is forewarned when
Parishioners call.
There are papers all over the desk, still.
Sealed envelopes that look like bills
He could not bear to open.
David the nice accountant may sort them now
I hope.
He seems to be round a lot.
Have we gone into receivership?

There are proofs of Dad's funeral service,
Dad's diary
The Parson's Pocket Book.
For tomorrow, I see he has written in his tiny scrawl
'Funeral at three."
He will not be taking that one, then.

I hope someone informed the relatives.

We have lived an old way,
With our six-acre garden
A Georgian Rectory
No money
And a wing and a prayer.

We will have to move house.
This room will take some cleaning.
There are Dad's treasures;
His lute, Dowland songs and a dusty viola.
Our earliest years were accompanied
By lute
Or guitar strings, then
Mum's calm
Harmonious Blacksmith.
I hear him near
Still playing softly in the shadows.

Our old London taxi may go.
Gar and Grandpapa have offered to buy
A new car.
A relief for Mum
As the old cab is cumbersome on country lanes,
Though convenient for a cello.
And cannot go faster than forty.

When you drown
Your body is puffed up,
Bloated, hard to recognise.
Dad had hoped to give his
To medical science,
But apparently they have no use
For the drowned.

After the Bishop left on Thursday
Mum said
"Did I kiss him goodbye?"
"The Bishop?"
"No, Daddy." And we said
"You did Mum.
You got up early to see us all off
You kissed him.

We saw."

A long, pale, slim coffin
New beech wood,
No mystery,
No ghosts.
It was just me and a dead man
In front of the rood screen,
Under the hammer beam angels.

In the study with his things, I expect
Dad to burst in and to grin at me,

Tell me he's late for something,
His own requiem, even.
Rush out again.
When we were ill and mum was at work
He might forget to feed us,
Dashing in mid-afternoon
When we dawned on him,
To make us black toast
Spread inedibly thick
With Marmite.

He has died.
"Well most people have, you know."
I picture him grinning diffidently as he quotes
C.S.Lewis.
Dad had Faith in the
Life Hereafter.
He may even have believed, like J.M Barrie
That death is
An adventure.

They are all in the church,
Praying from Dad's
Book of Catholic Devotions.
Go forth upon your journey Christian Soul
Go from this world.
I don't want Dad to
Go Forth.
I want him to be here,
Enjoying the funeral with us.

Another shore

We did not wear black.
We are not the sort of girls to own
Beaded hats and chic skirts
In readiness.
Alice and I pull on our cassocks
With the rest of the choir
And join the longest imaginable
Procession witnessed this century
In that massive, lovely old place
Dad tried so hard to fill,
Each week.

There's a wideness in God's Mercy
Like the wideness
Of the Sea.

People supposed we chose this hymn
For the reference to sea.
But it just happened to be one of his favourites
And fitted with his
Broad minded
Broad shouldered ways,
With a very strong tune

For a man to die in such
Sure and Certain Hope

Brings its own legacy.
We move up the aisle
On a wave of love and care
Clouds and darkness banished
By purpose,
Or so it feels in the moment.
Kevin is playing the organ.
A tall order for Kevin at just seventeen
He is up to it.

We have passed every
Wide spaced, beetle eaten pew.
Turning into the choir stalls
I notice Alastair.
Dad taught him to serve at Communion.
Lately, he has taken to visiting on his bike
For intense discussions with Dad in the study.
He still can't join choir
Because of his boarding school term.
Face whiter than his chasuble,
Sunset hair, slim and reedy these days,
He stands statue-like by the altar
Gripping a candle.

The Bishop places helpful emphasis on
Entering into
Eternal Life.
We sing
Christ has opened Paradise.

I hope they let Dad in.

You see
Paradise was here,
In Cawston Church,
Through the gate,
Into the garden
Where the angel led Dad in his dream.

At the end
We file after Dad's coffin.
Grandpapa reads in his
Deep, sure church voice
"Lord Now lettest thou thy servant depart in peace
According to thy word."

These words for a moment,
Thy Word,
According to It,
Just for a moment I felt
Like the time when the Angels sang
Through Kevin and Sylvia and Graham
In our church,
Hope sure and certain,
Golden wires meeting,
Heaven and earth,
Immortal hearts.

"Harps, Jess."

Oh yes, harps.

For a moment
Golden
With perfect words.

Then we file out of church
Kevin playing Finlandia
Haltingly.
Past our gate.
Up the path and out on to
New Street.
Past all the bungalows
Over the crossroads
Down to the cemetery.
The Tubbys and Tuddenhams have drawn their curtains
In respect.
The Mace shop is closed.

We have chosen a plot set apart
To fit everyone round.
Mum, Alice and me on the far side,
The Bishop and Grandpapa ready to bury,
Everyone else looking back at us.

London Granny, Dad's Mum
Usually glamourous, dominant, buoyant and tall,
Today grey and small,

Old to me, for the very first time.
You don't bury your son.
Our Aunt Thirza stands strong and impassive.
You don't bury your little brother.

Strength and light have gone,
Here in the straggly drab cemetery
Backing onto the Bowling Green.
I feel awkward and ordinary
The sun has gone in.

"In the midst of life
We are in death."

Alice sniffs, rubs her nose with the sleeve
Of her surplice.

"Of whom may we seek for succour?"

There are people around to be sought
But for succour?
What is succour actually?
No Purcell setting,
No music at all.

Rebecca and Paul stand with their mum
By the yew tree.
Richard is closer,
Just opposite.
He scowls at the earth heaped up round the grave.

Tim holds his hand
Which looks natural.
You might never be too old
To hold hands
With your father.

He fleeth as it were a shadow

I love Richard
And Kevin
And Alastair.
I love all the boys that I know,
Which is three.
I could never tell them.
I love boys who love music
And church organs
Boys who can talk about Greek and Philosophy
To me
Even if I am quite dim.
We have no boys left in our family.
Perhaps I have unborn
Of my own?
Girls too,
Of my own
One day?
Might they be children of one of these boys?
Dad will have grandchildren
But not hold them on earth
And not know.

Mum will know.
Mum will live a long time,
I am hoping.
Don't let Mum die.
Strange to be thinking of birth
As we bury Dad.

We Commit Dad's body to the ground.
People drift back to the Rectory
In need of a drink, now.
"Would you mind if I walk, Mum?"
"Of course you can walk, darling."
Mum understands.
She has looked inexpressibly weary
But today she has seemed to draw succour
From everyone's presence.
If that's what it means.

"Hello"
"Alastair!"
"So many people here

Such a great tribute to Paul", he says.
"Yes."
"Who is the boy with the shiny brown hair?"
"That's Richard.
He saved my life,
I don't know how to talk to him."
"You'll find a way, Jess.

Your father was handsome
So handsome, exotic,
Not like other people."
"Exotic?"
"I thought so. He taught me so much."
"Did he?"
I am not surprised,
Dad was good with teenagers.
Alice and I just beginning
To shine in his eyes
Alastair is fifteen now.
"What did you talk about?"
"Carpentry, Church, Early Music, relationships.
We talked for hours."

We had reached the Rectory drive
Down which people were piling.
"Come this way."

I pull Alastair by the hand,
Drag him round
To the side of the Church Hut
Where earlier hundreds of clergy had robed.
We edge our way
Into the orchard,
Still able to see the procession of
Wake attenders
Mercifully apart from them.
I have not let go of his hand

But grip it more tightly.
"This is where we used to play,"
I say, not awkward with Alastair.
Our childhood in this garden
Is over now
Anyway.

We have come up against a brick shack
"Who could forget?" says Alastair
"This, unless I'm much mistaken
Is base camp for
The Pigsty Regiment."
"You remember!"
"Of course.
"You Rectory kids always had the best games."
Alastair flops down on the grass by the pigsty,
We watch people flock into the Rectory.
No one would think to look over at us.

"I got told off for fidgeting
As your dad's coffin came up the aisle."
"You were still as a stone. I watched you."
"Did you? Well never mind.

Mr Bramble must be devastated."
"Yes, he loved Dad."
"Tears were dropping off his whiskers in the cemetery."
"Poor Mr Bramble."

"This would have been a great place for pigs
In the days of the Reverend Marsh or before."
"Did Mr Kett teach you about Revered Marsh?
And the rare fairy foxgloves?"
Alastair smiled.
"Mr Kett taught us everything. Started us off."
"He was different from Dad."
"So different."

"Perfect place for a pigsty
Fallen fruit from the orchard
To forage about in.
I do like the intelligent ways of the pig,
Though sheep are my first love."

"It used to be rabbits."

"Oh, you remember!"
"Might you come and see my sheep some time next holiday,
When I'm back from school?"
"Now there's an offer."
"And can I write to you?
Will you be alright, Jess?"
Oh fuck, how can you answer that?

We do not kiss
But I mention this
Because it felt as though we might have
If this had been someone else's life.

I stare at him for a moment
Quite overwhelmingly grateful
For his care.
"I'll miss you while you are at school,"
I say truthfully, having never missed him for one second
Before today.
"I'll be home again soon."

We sit for a little while longer
In the sun
Like basking pigs.
Then go in to join
Dad's funeral tea.

Patty starts up a game of volleyball
Which saves us from talking to people.
I see Alastair talking to Richard
And Kevin with Jenny from choir
Sitting together on the wall.
She is very pretty, after all.
Alice and Gar handing round sausage rolls,
Grandpapa crumbles one absent-mindedly onto the floor
In polite conversation with an eager young vicar.
I think people are having quite a good afternoon
All things considered.

I am back in my own bedroom now.
Since Dad has been buried
He is less likely to stray.

People die and we bury them
Restore order.
We have lived through
An in-between time
All this week
In the Rectory.
Sometimes Dad has seemed to be with us.
Now he has
Gone forth on his journey
We are told.
Is this something we can know?
It feels more like journey's end.
And where are the angels?

Before she took Granny back to London,
Thirza sought me out.
Her brother died.
I don't know what to say to her.
With Thirza no small talk is needed.
No talk at all, if you don't want to speak.
She and Dad differed that way.
Dad was chatty.

"Jess, our own father died when I was fifteen.
I was older than you and I would not presume
To know how you and Alice are feeling.
But here is your birthday present and it may help
To write some things down."

A soft red leather book with gold lettering,
A page for each year, stretching into the distance.
Diary of a Lifetime.

So life goes on, then?

"Thank you, Thirza. Thank you so much."
For knowing and being.
Thank you for aunts and their differing ways
Of loving.

What happens next?

Not where will we live
And how shall we cope
Mum will cope valiantly
She who would valiant be.
Caring and loving and
Seeking to minimise loss
All her life.

People will help
In their well-wishing way
And aunts who won't need explanations
But hold Dad in their own precious memories
Will help Mum to care for us.
And we will grow up without Dad
Who was…
How do you say what a Dad is?
Measure the lack of one

Over a lifetime?

And how do you shout about death in the sea
When even a whisper disturbs?
Even in a loving family
Who want to know,
Want to help,
Want to love.

It is too much.
We would lose the balance of our minds
Without the guard that comes down to protect us.
We would be flooded,
Our minds would drown in the sea.

One way is writing, perhaps?
And one way is music.
Music endures like
Immortal hearts.
Golden wires touch our heart strings
Speak
Unbearable pain-joy
And memory
Spills from our souls
As we sing.

The robin performs a cadenza
On an Arthur Bramble branch
Then high in the yew tree.

"Is that your story, child of yesterday?"

"Are you an angel, little robin?"

"Of course" says the robin. "You knew all along".

A man led his little family
To a Norfolk village
After a dream.

Time in paradise spent
On both sides of this gate
Before

A storm
And then

An angel pulled his boat
Up the farther shore
And led him home.

The family were stranded
Without him
They adapted
They accommodated their loss

As people do

And the dark and dreadful
The fear
The unbearable love

And all happiness
Is contained
Here by this gate
In this place
And every place
Now and forever.

"And all shall be well?"

The robin is gone.

I acknowledge with love and gratitude everyone in this book, especially my brilliant sister, Alice Farnham.

Thank you Alastair Boag and Jo Crocker for lifelong friendship, grown from shared Cawston roots.

I am deeply indebted to friends Caroline McGhie, Richard Girling and James Buckhalter for their professional wisdom.

Thank you loving cousins Louise and Peter Sollars who accompanied me back to Cawston, to Neal Gething for consummate listening and to Christine Dix who shared a glimpse of heaven.

Thank you Stephen Fry for the generosity of your introduction. And for being Dad's dear friend and teaching us so patiently.

Thank you to our wondrous children.

And to the Royal National Lifeboat Institution, without whom we would not be.

The publisher gratefully acknowledges Faber and Faber Ltd for granting permission to reproduce lines from *Four Quartets* by T.S. Eliot.

Thanks to Rebecca Pinner for permission to reproduce her photographs of the Cawston Angels.

'*Cawston Church*' reproduced from an original watercolour by Anthony B Butler in the author's private collection.

Photographs of Cawston Church and gate by Joanna Millington.